Wild Flower

Luciana Ftoni

BookLeaf
Publishing

India | USA | UK

Made with ❤ on the BookLeaf Publishing Platform
www.bookleafpub.in
www.bookleafpub.com

Dedication

To my mom,
who sees me as a poetic writer.

"She walks in beauty, like the night."
-Lord Byron

Preface

Acknowledgements

To my family, thank you. My mom, my dad, my siblings, thank you. My husband, Brian, for his love and support. My son, Micky-Lavender who brings out the inspiration and unconditional love. My friends for their enthusiasm and reviews. Community whom we share and exchange poetic language with. BookLeaf Publishing, thank you. You, the reader, it has been a pleasure putting this together for you to read and enjoy. All my love.

Then and Now

I have loved I have believed
therefore, I continue to love and believe.

Hurt

I could not see until I had hurt you
now that I can see
I am sorry I hurt you
I hope you can feel the love
instead of the hurt caused.

To Love

How nice is it
I get the chance to let you know
I love you
as I look into your eyes.

4

Abundance

Let it be a reminder of the abundance around you
everything you need there is plenty and more
everything you want comes your way as needed.

Roses

There is death in roses
even if *roses never die.*

Baby Boy

Having a baby is so much fun
his cheer
his laughter
his playful ways
is the way life intended
musical, artistic and creative
so much fun
it is true
this is joy
this sweet baby boy.

Rose Pink

I'd rather see the world in pink
blushing, kind, sweet, and pretty
keeping the summer sunset
light rose pink shades on.

Edgar Allen Poe

Poetry you love the good
you love the depressed
you speak to the heart
bring out the broken
poetry sets me free
the way it has me feeling part of society
deep on a gloomy rainy day
to use the grey as inspiration.

High Notes

Angelic Beauty Calm
Dreamy Excellence Favored
Grace Highness Idyllic
Joy Kind Lavender
Mindful Novel Original
Quiet Radiant Sage
Tender Universe
Vibrant Wise
Xylophone Yoga
Zen

Gratitude List

I believe in all the good things happening
blessings and health
son's smile and laugh
parents' travels
uber work
sisters' phone call
brother's "I love you." text
grocery shopping
husband's journal gift
the endless surprises
the blessings of the unknown
an exciting way to keep going.

Dalí Loved Gala

I love you
I love you
I love you
it just so happens
I love you
reminders of life
reminders say
I love you
I love you lovely I love you friendly
I love you art I love you especially
my apparition
my imagination
my dream work
awakening my senses
my kundalini
opening my mind
you are my search my longing

my peace my disturbance
my acceptance my reality
asking you to love me
the way Dali loved Gala.

Old Age

I like the old
old people seem to make everything last longer.

Judgement

The ones I do not know, I cannot judge
the ones I do know
I can make a judgment for myself.

Voice

Your voice has the perfect frequency
the perfect melody
sending positive vibrations to my eardrums
sounds making out
"Momma, I love you."

October's Sunset

My mind
my mind
a wandering mind of a wander
going places as the sunset falls in bliss for the evening of
tonight's charm
from elegant shifts of lavender, rose-colored clouds to
the dimmed light concluding the evening with orange
browns
nearly Fall-brown, to take off into the midnight blue of
this evening
low crescent moon
shadowing everything the eye knows to the unknown
thoughts we tend to hide during the daylight.

Blue partner

Fascinating each day I rise
fascinating to know blue partner rises
in all of its happiness and the grand scheme of things
the glory of the day seizes us with its blue sky above.

Even during the storm
blue partner is only a few hues away
from its apparition
sun salutation reaching up to the sky
praise
loving to be here the blue partner shines upon us
play your day as you wish
when all of a sudden eyes up above
all the things that come to mind.

Fun as it is not much gets in the way
the sky is opened in limitless ways

blue partner above
yes to the opened air
inhaling, exhaling
a reminder to the reader
take your moment
inhaling, exhaling
smiling
looking up at blue partner
feeling great
we all get to share the opened-air
yes, yes another day
blue partner here to stay.

Yes, the greatness of today
my spirit is in its oh most delight
with the bright light blue partner above.

Yoga

The practice of yoga asks:

Can you be kind when there is no kindness?
Can you be still in chaos?
Can you be patient in temper?
Can you bring light in darkness?

Work

People are working tirelessly while we rest
while we rest up I remember why I work tirelessly
all work done with love is bound to be successful.

Nature's Senses

Vision is a sunset
hearing the breeze
softly whispering
smell of cool air
touch of petals
taste of fresh citrus fruit.

Life is Beautiful

The birds
the trees
the bees
flower blooms
the child laughs
a smile
harmony
life is beautiful
hearing this song
as if the birds were singing for me
the world is humming my tune.

Reading

And so I am fearless through the strength of reading
and so I am understanding through the clarity of reading
and so I am wiser through the wisdom of reading
and so I am clean through the organization of reading
through reading
I uphold the psychic powers
of the past future and present
to live up to our highest expectations
of love and kindness the world asks of us.

www.ingramcontent.com/pod-product-compliance
Lightning Source LLC
Chambersburg PA
CBHW071245140726
47996CB00007B/2760